# Wartime Cookbook

## Food and Recipes from the Second World War 1939-45

### Anne and Brian Moses

Wayland

## Titles in this series

## The War Years: The Home Front
## Wartime Cookbook

**Picture acknowledgements**
The publisher would like to thank the following for allowing their pictures to be reproduced in this book: Hulton Deutsch 38 bottom; Imperial War Museum cover: top centre and right, title page 6 bottom, 7, 8, 9 top, 10, 11 both, 12 both, 13, 14 both, 15, 16, 18, 20, 21, 22, 28, 29, 30, 33, 32 both, 39, 40, 43, 45; Peter Newark's Historical Pictures cover top left, 5, 9 bottom, 25, 26 both, 36 top; Popperfoto 24, 42; Topham Picture Library 4 both, 6 top, 17, 19, 23 both, 27, 31 both, 34, 35, 36 bottom, 37, 38 top, 41, 44 both. The artwork was supplied by Jenny Hughes.

**Cover:** (bottom) a typical week's wartime food ration for one person; (top left) a 'Dig for Victory' campaign poster; (top centre) putting waste food in a pig bin; (top right) a government poster encouraging people to grow and preserve their own food.
**Title page:** a Guernsey family enjoying a victory meal.

**Series editor:** Francesca Motisi
**Book editor:** Joanne Jessop
**Designer:** Malcolm Walker
**Picture researchers:** Shelley Noronha & Brian Moses
**Production controller:** Carol Titchener

First published in 1995 by
Wayland (Publishers) Limited
61 Western Road
Hove, East Sussex, BN3 1JD
England

© Copyright 1995 Wayland (Publishers) Limited

**British Library Cataloguing in Publication Data**
Moses, Brian
    Wartime Cookbook: Food and Recipes from the
Second World War. 1939–45
    I. Title
    641.5941

ISBN 0–7502–1633–6

Typeset by Kudos Editoroial and Design Services
Printed and bound by B.P.C. Paulton Books, Great Britain

# Contents

# Why Rationing?

On 1 September 1939, German troops marched into Poland. Two days later, Britain and France declared war against Germany and the Second World War began. The war was to last for the next six years.

Before the war started, Britain imported two thirds of its food. But once the war had started, ships and their crews were in danger from German bombs and torpedoes, so fewer ships were bringing food to Britain. Soon imported food was in short supply.

**Above** A newspaper seller in London on 1 September 1939.

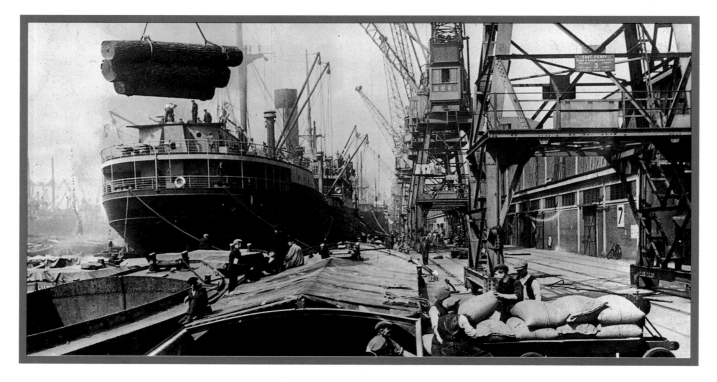

**Above** Before the war, two thirds of Britain's food was brought in by ships from other countries around the world.

The government started a system of food rationing to make sure that everyone received a fair share of the limited supplies of food. Without rationing, it was possible that people with extra money would buy up large amounts of scarce items, such as sugar or tea, while others went without.

Before rationing began, there was some panic buying as people tried to hoard food in preparation for the tough times ahead.

*Since the declaration of war, many people have been laying in additional stocks of food, particularly sugar and tinned meats . . . So great has been the demand for sugar, in particular, that many shops have placed a restriction on the amount that may be bought by any one customer.*

Falkirk Herald
*9 September 1939*

**Above** This war poster shows the dangers faced by the crews who sailed the ships bringing food and other supplies into Britain. The people of Britain were very thankful that the men of the merchant navy were willing to risk their lives to keep the supply lines open.

## APPLE JELLY

Peel, core and cut ½ lb (225g) of apples. Put the apples into a saucepan, cover with water and simmer until tender. Sweeten with 1 dessertspoon of honey and flavour with cinnamon or ginger. Whip the mixture until it is light and frothy. Dissolve ½ tablet of jelly in ¼ pint (125 ml) of hot water. Let it cool then mix with the apple mixture. Leave to set overnight in the fridge.

# How Rationing Worked

In September 1939, a new government department called the Ministry of Food was set up to organize and to oversee food rationing. The new Ministry declared 19 September as National Registration Day. On this day, each householder had to fill in a form giving the names of all the people living in the house. Local Food Offices used this information to prepare ration books, which were sent out to everyone. People were asked to register with the grocer and butcher where they intended to buy their rationed food.

Rationing started on 8 January 1940. After that date, when people bought rationed food they handed in coupons from their ration books to the shopkeeper.

**Above** Wartime ration books.

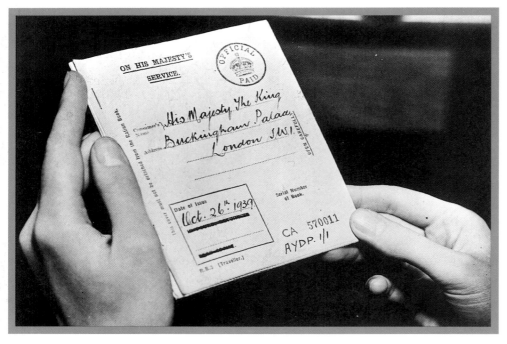

Each person in the country, rich or poor, needed a food ration book. Even King George VI had a ration book.

## LORD WOOLTON'S VEGETABLE PIE

This recipe was named after the popular Minister for Food, Lord Frederick Woolton.

2 lb (1 kg) potatoes
1 lb (450 g) cauliflower
1 lb (450 g) carrots
½ lb (225 g) swede
½ lb (225 g) parsnips
3 or 4 spring onions
water for cooking
1 teaspoon (5 ml) vegetable extract
1 tablespoon (15 ml) oatmeal
chopped parsley
2 oz (50 g) grated cheese

Cook half the potatoes, the vegetables, the vegetable extract and oatmeal for 10 minutes in enough water to cover them. Stir occasionally to prevent sticking. Cool and place in a pie dish. Sprinkle with chopped parsley. Boil, then mash the rest of the potatoes; spread them over the vegetables to make a crust. Sprinkle the cheese on top. Bake at 190°C, 375°F, gas mark 5 until lightly browned. Serve with gravy and vegetables. Serves 6–8.

A shopkeeper stamps a customer's coupons. That person was then allowed to buy all the tea, sugar, butter, margarine, cooking fats and bacon that was allowed to each person for one week.

There were three kinds of ration books: a general book for people over 6 years old; a child's book for those under 6; and a special traveller's book for workers such as lorry drivers who travelled around the country.

The first food items to be rationed were butter, sugar and bacon and ham. The weekly allowances per person were 4 oz (100 g) of butter, 12 oz (350 g) of sugar, and 4 oz (100 g) of bacon and ham.

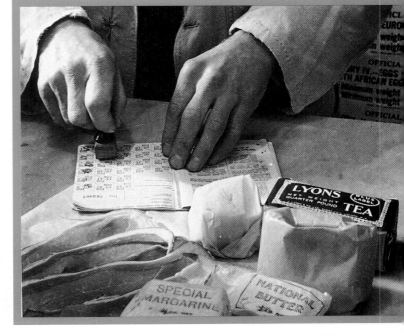

# Making Do with Less

In March 1940, all types of meat were rationed. Each person over 6 years old was entitled to 1 shilling and 10 pence (9p in today's money) worth of meat; children under 6 were entitled to 11 pence worth (less than 5p in today's money). By July, tea was on the ration books, at 2 oz (50 g) per week, and cooking fats and margarine, at 2 oz (50 g). The sugar ration was cut to 8 oz (225 g) per week.

A typical week's rations for one adult.

*I hated everything being on ration. In the morning we used to get up and my Mum always used to be making porridge. But because sugar was on ration it tasted horrible, and it tasted worse if you put salt on it. Then I remember Mum finding a tin of syrup in the cupboard and instead of having sugar on porridge we had syrup and it was delicious.*
Children of the Blitz *by Robert Westall*

## MACARONI AND BACON DISH

$\frac{1}{2}$ oz (12.5 g) dripping, or other fat
2 oz (50 g) leek or onion, peeled and chopped
2 oz (50 g) bacon, chopped
1 pint (500 ml) vegetable stock, made by dissolving a vegetable
    stock cube in boiling water
6 oz (150 g) macaroni
salt and pepper

Melt the dripping in a pan and fry the leek and bacon until lightly browned. Add the stock, bring to the boil, and add the macaroni and seasoning. Cook for 20 minutes or until the macaroni is tender and the water is absorbed. Garnished with watercress. Serves 4.

**Above** A wartime cooking demonstration put on by the Ministry of Food.

**Right** A newspaper article published by the Ministry of Food describing new ways to cook salt fish.

A points system was introduced in 1941. People were allowed 16 points per month, in addition to their weekly rations. The points could be 'spent' on luxury foods such as dried fruit, biscuits, cereals, tinned fish and meat. Each of these foods was given a point value; for example, 2 lb (1 kg) of dried fruit was worth 16 points. Any luxury food that became scarce would have its point value raised; and if there was plenty, its point value would be lowered.

The Ministry of Food published 'Food Facts' in the newspapers to help people make the most of their rationed food. 'Kitchen Front' radio broadcasts and 'Food Flashes' on cinema screens gave information and advice on preparing interesting and nutritious meals from available foods.

# Dig for Victory

*Dig! Dig! Dig! And your muscles will grow big,*
*Keep on pushing the spade!*
*Don't mind the worms,*
*Just ignore their squirms,*
*And when your back aches laugh with glee*
*And keep on diggin'*
*Till we give our foes a wiggin'*
*Dig! Dig! Dig! to victory.*

Popular wartime song

The 'Dig for Victory' campaign was a great success. People dug up their lawns and flower beds to make vegetable gardens. Those without gardens grew lettuces, radishes and even runner beans in window boxes. Golf courses were dug up, and bomb sites and rubbish tips were dug over to create garden space. Vegetables were grown in parks, around the edges of football pitches, on the sides of railway embankments and on grass verges.

There were allotments in city parks and even in the moat around the Tower of London.

### MARROW PUDDING

Boil a small marrow or half a large marrow in water and strain through a colander. Fill a pie dish three-quarters full with the marrow. Add a lump of butter and a little sugar and spice for flavouring. Fill up the dish with milk and bake on an oven tray for 45 minutes at 190°C, 375°F, gas mark 5. Serves 4.

*Of course all the vegetables were ready to eat at the same time. We couldn't possibly eat them all at once and there were no such things as freezers . . . My mother had to spend hours bottling vegetables and fruit in large glass Kilner jars for us to eat in the winter months.*

We Were There in the 1940s
*by Rosemary Rees*

People grew food on every available piece of land. They even planted vegetables in the earth that covered their Anderson bomb shelters.

11

# Wartime Farming

**Above** Land girls working a new potato planter.

**Right** Woman were encouraged to take farm jobs.

Farm animals took up valuable land space and ate crops that could be eaten by people. The Ministry of Agriculture asked farmers to kill many of their sheep and cattle and plough up grazing fields to grow food. Farmers were asked to 'Plough Now! By Day and Night.'

The Women's Land Army was set up to encourage women to work on the farms. The 80,000 'Land Girls', as they were called, worked extremely hard for very little money. The 40,000 Italian and German prisoners of war were also set to work on the land.

Come and help with the

## VICTORY HARVEST

You are needed in the fields!

APPLY TO NEAREST EMPLOYMENT EXCHANGE FOR LEAFLET & ENROLMENT FORM OR WRITE DIRECT TO THE DEPARTMENT OF AGRICULTURE FOR SCOTLAND 15 GROSVENOR STREET, EDINBURGH.

lend a hand on the land

at a farming holiday camp

Many children were persuaded to 'lend a hand on the land' by joining 'Help a Farmer' schemes at weekends and during the school holidays.

Wartime farming was very productive. There was a great increase in the use of farm machinery, such as the potato planter shown on page 12. Crop planting more than doubled and wartime harvests were at record levels.

### PARSNIP PUDDING
Mash 2 medium-sized cooked cold parsnips with a tablespoon of cocoa. Add a pinch of bicarbonate of soda. Warm $1/2$ pint (250 ml) of milk and sweeten with sugar or sweetener. Add the milk to the parsnip mixture and mix together. Bake for 30 minutes at 190°C, 375°F, gas mark 5. Serves 4.

# Doctor Carrot

DOCTOR CARROT
the Children's best friend

VIT-A

**Left** Doctor Carrot was a familiar character to wartime children. He reminded them of how important it was to eat plenty of carrots.

**Below** People were also encouraged to eat plenty of green vegetables as a substitute for raw fruit, which was often not available.

Doctor Carrot, who was a cartoon character dreamed up by the Ministry of Food, told people about the value of carrots. One of Doctor Carrot's messages was that eating lots of carrots, which contain Vitamin A, would help people to see better during the blackout. In fact, it would take a vast quantity of carrots to improve night vision. Nevertheless, Doctor Carrot had plenty of good ideas for interesting carrot recipes. One of the strangest was carrot marmalade, but not everyone appreciated it.

**GREEN VEGETABLES & SALADS**
help you to resist infection, clear the skin, and take the place of raw fruit.

## CARROT COOKIES

1 tablespoon (15 ml) margarine
2 tablespoons (30 ml) sugar
a few drops vanilla, almond or orange flavouring
4 tablespoons (60 ml) grated raw carrot
6 tablespoons (90 ml) self-raising flour, or plain flour and
 $\frac{1}{2}$ teaspoon (2.5 ml) baking powder
extra sugar to sprinkle on top of the cookies

Cream the margarine and sugar together until light and fluffy.
Beat in the flavouring and grated carrot. Fold in the flour, or
flour and baking powder. Drop spoonfuls of the mixture into
small greased patty pans. Sprinkle the tops with the extra sugar
and bake at 220°C, 425°F, gas mark 7 for about 20 minutes.
Makes 12 to 15 cookies.

*One morning a jar was put on the breakfast table . . . My
father . . . spread the nectar on his bread and bit into it. He
frowned and said: 'What was that?'*
*'Carrot marmalade,' said my mother.*
*With unusual deliberation . . . he picked up the jar, took it
into the garden and poured it on the compost heap.*

The Sheltered Days *by Derek Lambert*

'Victory' dishes that were
made from vegetables
and other non-imported
foods on sale at a
London restaurant.

# Potato Pete

The Ministry of Food recommended eating potatoes twice a day. There were several reasons for this. Eating more potatoes meant that people ate less bread, which in turn meant that less wheat had to be imported to make flour. Potatoes were also considered to be a healthy food and a good source of Vitamin C, which helps to fight off infection.

There were recipes for using potatoes in pastry, rissoles, puddings, sandwiches and cakes. A cartoon character called Potato Pete was invented to promote potatoes. He even had his own song.

*Potato Pete, Potato Pete,*
*See him coming down the street,*
*Shouting his good things to eat,*
*'Get your hot potatoes*
   *from Potato Pete.'*

The cartoon character Potato Pete was invented by the Ministry of Food to persuade people to eat more potatoes.

Schoolboys digging up potatoes as part of their lessons.

For those who still found it hard to cope with potato skins, the Ministry of Food once again had the answer.

*Dearly beloved brethren,*
*Is it not a sin,*
*To peel potatoes and to throw away the skin.*
*The skin feeds the pigs*
*And the pigs feed us.*
*Dearly beloved brethren is that not enough?*

## POTATO PIGLETS

This recipe was a tasty substitute for sausage rolls, although sausages were difficult to come by in wartime.

6 medium potatoes, well scrubbed
6 skinned sausages

Remove a centre core, using an apple corer, from the length of each potato. Stuff the hole with the sausage meat. Bake the stuffed potatoes for about an hour at 220°C, 400°F, gas mark 6. Serve on a bed of chopped cabbage – raw or cooked.

It can be difficult to core the potatoes. Ask an adult to help.

# Keeping Livestock

One way to get extra meat was to form a 'pig club'. A club might consist of several families or a number of factory workers; all the club members helped to feed a pig and then shared the meat when the pig was butchered. Pigs were raised in gardens and garages and even the empty cages at London Zoo.

London policemen, who formed a pig club, cleaning out the pig sty.

By 1943, there were nearly seven thousand clubs. Here is a report on the Hyde Park Police pig club:

*The sty that houses these important pigs was built by policemen, and built like a gaol. Evidently the police were afraid that the pigs might escape.*

Farmers' Weekly, *1941*

18

## LIVER SAVOURY

You can use any kind of liver for this recipe. Chop ¼ lb (100 g) liver into small pieces, coat them with flour and fry in dripping. Cover 4 slices of stale bread with sliced tomatoes, sprinkle with grated cheese, dot with little lumps of fat and grill quickly. Place the fried liver pieces on top of the grilled bread and serve.

Be sure to ask an adult to help you to chop and fry the liver and to use the grill.

Chickens were raised in back gardens and in sheds, on flat rooftops and on balconies in the middle of towns. Most hens provided a good supply of eggs. But when owners were told to 'weed out wasters', many found it hard to kill the chickens they had come to look on as family pets, and even harder to eat the meat that appeared on the table.

The Ministry of Food also encouraged people to keep rabbits, which were cheap to house and feed and a valuable substitute for beef.

Chickens raised in the back garden provided a good supply of off-ration eggs.

19

# Shortages

By the spring of 1941, more and more ships were being sunk by German U-boats in the Battle of the Atlantic. These heavy shipping losses meant that even less food was reaching Britain. In May, cheese was rationed for the first time, the small amount of rationed meat was often hard to find, and the butter ration was cut to 2 oz (50 g) a week.

The Ministry of Food reminded people not to waste bread because imported wheat took up a great deal of shipping space. People who wasted bread were sometimes taken to court and fined.

A mother measuring out food for her daughter's lunch. The chart on the wall was provided by the government and gives a guide to the amount of meat, potatoes, cheese and other foods needed for a healthy diet.

*Miss Mary Bridget O'Sullivan, Normandy Avenue, Herts, was fined a total of ten pounds, with two guineas [£2.10] costs, at Barnet today for permitting bread to be wasted. Her servant Miss Domenica Rosa Persi was fined five shillings [25p] for wasting bread.*

*It was stated that the servant was twice seen throwing bread to the birds in the garden, and when Miss O'Sullivan was interviewed she admitted that bread was put out every day. 'I cannot see the birds starve,' she said.*

Bristol Evening Post
*2 0 January 1943*

### CHEESE PUDDING

¹/₂ pint (250 ml) milk
2 eggs
4 oz (100 g) grated cheese
1 cup breadcrumbs
salt and pepper
¹/₄ teaspoon (1 ml) dried mustard

Mix the milk and eggs then stir in the other ingredients. Pour into a greased ovenproof dish and bake at 200°C , 400°F, gas mark 6 for 30 minutes or until brown and set. Serves 4.

A young girl puts kitchen waste into a pig bin. The scraps were then collected and fed to pigs.

Thoughtful families put their waste food in pig bins, which were collected and made into pig swill. As the Ministry of Food reminded everyone:

*Because of the pail, the
  scraps were saved,
Because of the scraps, the
  pigs were saved,
Because of the pigs, the
  rations were saved,
Because of the rations, the
  ships were saved,
Because of the ships, the
  island was saved,
Because of the island, the
  Empire was saved,
And all because of a
  housewife's pail.*

# Anti-Waste Campaign

Everyone was asked to save fuel during the war. Housewives were reminded that they were in the front line of the 'Battle for Fuel'. Here is some helpful advice from the Ministry of Power and Fuel:

*Never heat the oven for one cake or pudding, plan a baking day. Arrange with neighbours to share ovens, a cake might be baked while a casserole is slowly cooking or two joints of meat could be cooking at the same time.*

A clear plate means A clear conscience

Don't take more than you can eat

This wartime poster reminds people not to waste food by putting more on their plates than they can eat. To waste anything during the war years was frowned upon because all extra food and fuel was needed in the war effort.

This woman and her young child load coal into the pram after a long wait in a queue.

The Ministry of Power and Fuel also reminded housewives that the careful use of cinders to light fires in each home would save 750,000 tons of coal a year, which was the amount of coal needed to produce the steel for making 10 battleships.

The amount of gas and electricity allotted to each household was determined by the number of rooms in the house and the area of the country – the farther north, the more gas and electricity householders were allowed to use.

**Above** A boy collects firewood from bombed houses. One way to save coal was to burn wood.

### SKIRLY-MIRLY
Boil equal quantities of peeled potatoes and peeled swedes separately in salted water until tender. Drain well. Mash the potatoes and swedes into a smooth paste and mix well. Add a little hot milk and margarine to taste. Season with pepper. Serve piled in a hot vegetable dish.

# Strange Foods

*Best was American dried egg. You poured a thin trickle into the frying pan, then as it cooked it blew up like a balloon, till it was two inches thick, like a big yellow hump-backed whale.*

Children of the Blitz *edited by Robert Westall*

Hunting rabbits was one way of increasing the meat supply. These men have just returned from the hunt with their 'kill' of rabbits.

In 1942, dried egg powder appeared in the shops. Every 4 weeks, shoppers were allowed one 12-egg packet. A Ministry of Food leaflet did its best to promote dried eggs:

*Dried eggs are the complete hen's eggs, both white and the yolk, dried to a powder. Nothing is added. Nothing but the moisture and the shell is taken away, leaving the eggs themselves as wholesome, as digestible and as full of nourishment and health-promoting value as if you had just taken the eggs new laid from the nest.*

24

The search for unrationed food took people to the countryside to hunt for rabbits and look for wild birds' eggs. One woman recalls how she used to go 'guleging' – collecting gulls' eggs:

*We got a big bucketful each, and they were as big as ducks' eggs. You'd think they'd be fishy, but they're not . . . It was absolutely legal then but you wouldn't be allowed to take the eggs today.*

The Wartime Kitchen and Garden
*by Jennifer Davies*

Someone wrote to a Scottish newspaper to suggest using cormorants' eggs for baking cakes; the writer also claimed that roasted cormorant was quite tasty. One London restaurant that served any unrationed food it could get hold of once featured 'Roast Eagle and Veg' on its menu.

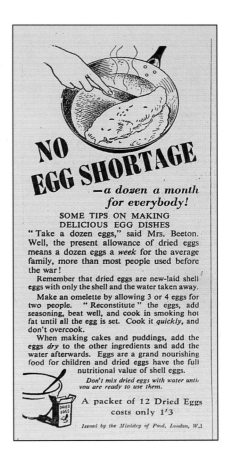

A notice published by the Ministry of Food in 1944 on the use of dried eggs.

## EGGLESS SPONGE

6 oz (150 g) self-raising flour
1 teaspoon (5 ml) baking powder
2½ oz (65 g) margarine
2 oz (50 g) sugar
1 tablespoon (15 ml) golden syrup
¼ pint (125 ml) milk or milk and water
jam for filling

Sift the flour and baking powder. Cream the margarine, sugar and golden syrup until soft and light, add a little flour then a little liquid. Continue like this until the mixture is smooth. Then grease and flour two 7-inch (18-cm) cake tins and divide the mixture between them. Bake in the centre of a moderately hot oven – 200°C, 400°F, gas mark 6 – for about 20 minutes or until firm to the touch. Allow the cake to cool slightly and then tip out of the tins. Spread jam on one cake and cover with the other cake to make a sandwich.

# Finding Substitutes

In 1941, when the Lend-Lease Agreement between the USA and Britain came into force, Britain began to import corned beef and spam to increase the meat rations.

In the last months of the war, whale meat was offered for sale, but few people liked its oily taste. It also came in tins as whale steak casserole, whale steak and kidney pudding and whale-meat roll. Tinned snoek (barracuda) – a large sea fish from the West Indies – was even less popular than whale meat.

**Above** A 1944 advertisement for spam. Spam was imported from the USA when the Lend-Lease Agreement came into force in 1941.

**Left** These children are being served a school dinner of American Lend-Lease bacon and eggs. Notice the menu posted on the blackboard.

26

## CORNED BEEF HASH

8 oz (225 g) corned beef
8 oz (225 g) cooked potatoes
8 oz (225 g) tomatoes
$^1/_2$ oz (15 g) dripping
2 medium-sized onions, peeled and grated
seasoning

Dice the corned beef and cooked potatoes. Slice the tomatoes. Melt the dripping in a frying pan, then add the onions and fry gently until soft. Add the diced corned beef and potatoes, cook for several minutes, then add the sliced tomatoes and a little seasoning. Cover the pan with a lid or plate and cook very slowly for 15 minutes. Serves 4.

Remember to ask an adult to help when chopping and frying food.

When the Channel Islands were invaded and occupied by German troops in 1940, food became increasingly scarce. The islanders experimented with all kinds of substitute foods. They collected carrageen moss (a frilly seaweed) from the beaches, washed and dried it several times then mixed it with milk to make a kind of blancmange. They used acorns, parsnips, wheat, sugar beet or lupin seeds to make a substitute coffee, and made tea from dried bramble leaves or grated and dried carrots.

These women are packing tins with whale-meat roll. Although most people did not like the oily taste of whale meat, it did have some advantages. It was unrationed and off the point system, so people could buy as much whale meat as they liked.

# Fruits of the Countryside

The countryside provided plenty of free and unrationed food, so people were encouraged to gather fruits, berries and fungi from hedgerows and woods. Teams of children with their parents or groups of Brownies and Cubs with their leaders would set out to collect nuts, blackberries, crab apples, wild mushrooms, dandelion leaves, stinging nettles and rosehips.

*I was one of these harvesters . . . Every autumn weekend, groups from school fanned out over North Devon, ploughing up hill and down dale, drenched or burnt by the sun, and bitten by every insect known to our biology mistress. Stained like Ancient Britons due to steady sampling, we picked for hours, our backs breaking in the search for the tiny bilberries hidden at ground level, and which the school cook made into jam.*

Talking about the War *by Anne Valery*

People from towns and cities travelled out to the countryside to pick berries and nuts, and any other food they could find.

Magazines provided recipes and helpful hints for using food gathered on trips to the countryside. Here is one interesting example:

*A poached egg on a bed of dandelion or nettle purée covered with cheese sauce is an almost perfect meal.*
Kitchen Front Recipes and Hints *by Ambrose Heath*

These women are making jam from berries that were picked in the countryside.

### NETTLE TEA
Gather young stinging nettles. Remember to put on an old pair of gloves for picking. Wash and dry the nettles in the sun. When dry, crumble up and boil in water to draw out the flavour. Nettle tea once a day makes a good, healthy drink.

# The Evacuees

At various times throughout the war, children were evacuated from Britain's cities and sent to live with foster parents in safe areas of the countryside. Many of these evacuees came from overcrowded homes in city slums and were infested with lice and suffering from skin diseases. Often these children missed the sort of food that they ate at home.

Host families were amazed when slum children refused porridge for breakfast and asked instead for bread and lard. Many were used to fish and chips for dinner and eel pie, cockles and winkles or cheese and beer for supper.

Evacuee children being fed at school.

## TOAD-IN-THE-HOLE

4 oz (100 g) plain flour
pinch of salt
1 egg or 1 tablespoon (15 ml) dried egg
$\frac{1}{2}$ pint (250 ml) milk (or milk and water mixed)
$\frac{1}{2}$ oz (15 g) lard
10–12 thin pork sausages

Make a pouring batter by mixing together the flour, salt, egg and milk. Put the sausages in a Yorkshire pudding tin (about 25 by 30 cm) greased with lard and cook for 5 or 10 minutes at 230°C, 440°F, gas mark 7. When the fat starts to run out of the sausages, pour in the batter and bake for 35 minutes, until the batter is risen and well browned. Serves 4.

Remember to ask an adult to help you when you are using a hot oven.

30

These evacuee children are enjoying a meal at their new home in the countryside. Some evacuee children had a much healthier diet in their foster homes.

A survey at the time found that many of the evacuees were not used to sitting down for a meal but 'seemed to like the food in the hand'. It was reported that two boys tried to eat soup with a knife and fork and that few children would eat food that needed chewing.

Some children were miserable in their new homes, but others welcomed the changes.

*We never had breakfast in Stepney Green, just a cup of tea and a slice of bread. There we were, in a shining little room that smelled of polish, and a table all set out with knives and forks and marmalade. And we were eating soft-boiled eggs. Well, if this was evacuation I was all for it.*

The World Is a Wedding
*by Bernard Kops*

MILK THE BACKBONE OF YOUNG BRITAIN

Posters like the one shown here reminded mothers of the importance of milk in their children's diets. Many children from the poorer parts of Britain were not used to drinking milk.

# The Nation's Health

When the war began, almost half the population of Britain was suffering from some degree of malnutrition. In the 1930s there had been unemployment and poverty on a huge scale, which meant that many families did not always have enough money to buy healthy food. Wartime food rationing helped to improve the health of the nation by keeping prices low enough for everyone to afford nutritious food. Food rationing actually improved most people's diet because they were forced to cut down on fatty foods, such as cheese, butter, lard, meat, and biscuits, and replace them with fresh vegetables and fruits, which were not rationed.

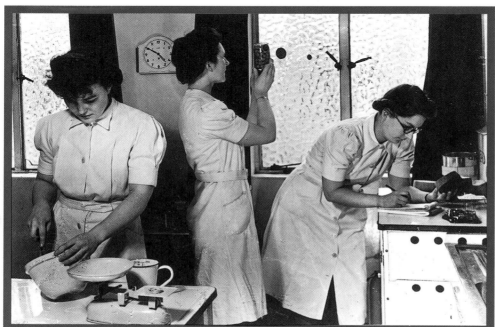

**Above** A war poster reminding mothers to give their babies cod- liver oil and orange juice. Orange juice became available from the USA after 1941.

**Left** Staff at work at one of the Ministry of Food's wartime kitchens. They worked out what nutrients were necessary for good health and how many calories were needed to work long hours.

## QUICK VEGETABLE SOUP

½ oz (15 g) dripping
12 oz (350 g) mixed vegetables, diced
1½ pints (750 ml) water or stock
salt and pepper
chopped parsley

Melt the dripping in a saucepan, add the vegetables and cook gently in the fat for at least 5 minutes. Add the liquid and simmer slowly for 25 minutes. Season the soup, then rub through a sieve to make a purée. Reheat and serve sprinkled with chopped parsley. Serves 4.

There was a growing awareness of the importance of healthy food for the general well-being of the nation. In order to win the war, people needed to be sufficiently well fed to work harder and longer than they did in peacetime.

> *Slowly the idea dawned that what you ate might actually affect your body. Before the war, we ate what was nice – fish and chips, sausages, pies, cakes, sweets – with hardly a green vegetable in sight.*
>
> Children of the Blitz *by Robert Westall*

During the war, people replaced rationed food, which was often very fatty with lots of fresh vegetables, which were not rationed and much healthier.

Children's diets were greatly improved. A 'Vitamin Welfare' scheme began in December 1941 with a free issue of black-currant juice and cod-liver oil for children under 2 years old. Milk was provided free to all pregnant women and children under 5 in those families with earnings below £2 per week. Many schools started providing meals during the war years.

# The Wheatmeal Loaf

*Pat-a-loaf, pat-a-loaf*
*Baker's Man*
*Bake me some Wheatmeal*
*As fast as you can:*
*It builds up my health*
*And its taste is so good,*
*I find that I like*
*Eating just what I should.*
        Popular wartime rhyme

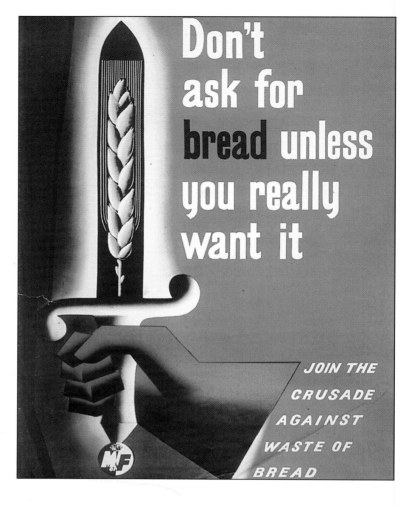

This wartime poster was used as part of the government's campaign to encourage people to eat less bread.

The National Wheatmeal Loaf, introduced in the autumn of 1942, was made with flour that contained nearly all the wheat grain, including the husks. The result was a heavy loaf with a gritty texture and a dirty beige colour, despite every effort to make it as white as possible. Even though this wheatmeal bread was much healthier, it was very unpopular with a nation used to eating only white bread. The National Wheatmeal Loaf was described as 'nasty, dirty, coarse, dark and indigestible'. But it was important to the war effort because using more of the grain to make flour meant that less wheat had to be imported.

When white flour was unavailable in the German-occupied Channel Islands, it was replaced with wholemeal flour that was often impure. As a result, it was not uncommon to find pieces of straw, string, fragments of gunnybag and even used matchsticks in a loaf of wholemeal bread.

## WELSH RAREBIT (USING STALE CRUSTS)

1½ oz (40 g) stale crusts, soaked in water and squeezed
4 tablespoons (60 ml) milk
2 oz (50 g) grated cheese
1 teaspoon (5 ml) mustard
1–2 teaspoons (15–30 ml) salt
pinch of pepper
½ oz (15 g) margarine
4 slices of toast

Mix the soaked bread with the milk, half the cheese and the seasoning. Beat well. Melt the margarine in a saucepan, then add the bread and cheese mixture and cook until hot and well blended. Spread it on the slices of toast and sprinkle with the remainder of the cheese. Brown gently under the grill. Serve very hot. Serves 4.

These people are having a simple restaurant meal with no bread. Notice the poster on the wall.

# The Black Market

Living with the wartime food restrictions could get extremely tiresome, so it was tempting to bend the law a bit if there was an opportunity to get hold of some extra rationed food such as meat or sugar. Throughout the war, there was a thriving black market in operation. Almost everyone 'knew a man' who could get hold of some scarce or rationed item, if the price was right. So for those who could afford it, and did not worry about breaking the law, extra food could always be found on the black market.

**Above** Wartime meals could become rather boring.

> *You'd probably hear that there'd be some sugar about somewhere, if you could find your way to it, which had 'fallen' off the back of a lorry. Pheasants 'came' out of trees too.*
> The Wartime Kitchen and Garden
> *by Jennifer Davies*

The dark streets during the black-out provided a good cover for thieves. As a result, there was an increase in thefts from warehouses during the war years.

This man is darkening the windows of the cafe to stop light from escaping during the blackout. During the blackout there was an increase in the number of thefts from warehouses. The food would then find its way on to the black market.

On a larger scale, rationed goods would go astray at the docks or railways. Here is what often happened:

> *The lorry would arrive in the docks for, say 100 sides of beef and the checker would ask him if he wanted some extras. If he was that way inclined he'd take 110, sign for 100 and then, on the way to Smithfield drop the extra lot off at a butcher's shop.*
>
> A People's War *by Peter Lewis*

Unloading a shipment of eggs from Australia. Food would sometimes go missing from the docks and later appear for sale on the black market.

Heavy fines – sometimes up to £500 plus two years' imprisonment – for anyone caught dealing in stolen goods helped to discourage black marketeering. As a result, the black market was not as big in Britain as it was in other European countries.

## CRUNCHIES

4 oz (100 g) margarine, lard or dripping
2 oz (50 g) sugar
2 oz (50 g) syrup
5 oz (125 g) plain flour
4 oz (100 g) medium oatmeal
1 teaspoon (5 ml) baking powder
vanilla flavouring

Cream together the fat, sugar and syrup. Add the flour, oatmeal, baking powder and a few drops of vanilla flavouring. Knead the mixture until it binds. Roll out the dough on a floured surface to about ¼ inch (1 cm) thickness. Cut into rounds or fingers. Bake at 180°C, 350°F, gas mark 4 on a greased oven tray for about 20 minutes or until golden brown. This recipe makes about 20 crunchies. They keep well stored in an air-tight tin.

# Sweet Things

Sweets were on ration at either 12 oz (300 g) or 8 oz (200 g) every four weeks, so 'sweetie coupons' were highly prized by children. Sometimes kind grandparents gave their sweets allowances to their grandchildren. Children liked to ask American soldiers, who were stationed in Britain after 1942, for candy and gum.

*When you could buy sweets they came wrapped in a cone of newspaper like fish and chips did. You tore the newspaper in half afterwards to use in the lavatory.*

When I Was Young
*by Neil Thomson*

**Above** This young girl is trying to decide how to spend her weekly sweet ration.

**Left** An American soldier giving away sweets that he and his friends had been saving from their own rations.

## UNCOOKED CHOCOLATE CAKE

2 oz (50 g) margarine
2 oz (50 g) sugar
2 tablespoons (30 ml) golden syrup
2 oz (50 g) cocoa powder
vanilla essence
6 oz (150 g) crisp breadcrumbs

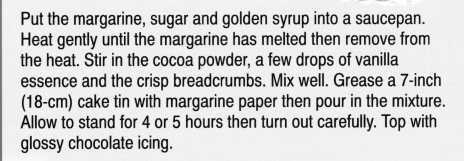

Put the margarine, sugar and golden syrup into a saucepan. Heat gently until the margarine has melted then remove from the heat. Stir in the cocoa powder, a few drops of vanilla essence and the crisp breadcrumbs. Mix well. Grease a 7-inch (18-cm) cake tin with margarine paper then pour in the mixture. Allow to stand for 4 or 5 hours then turn out carefully. Top with glossy chocolate icing.

To make the crisp breadcrumbs, bake some pieces of bread in the oven until crispy (do this when cooking another dish to save gas or electricity). Let the bread cool then crush it between pieces of greaseproof paper with a rolling pin or put in a blender. Ask an adult to help you use a blender.

## THE ICING

To make the glossy icing, mix together 2 teaspoons (10 ml) melted margarine, 1 tablespoon (15 ml) cocoa powder, 1 tablespoon (15 ml) golden syrup and a few drops of vanilla essence.

As the war went on, the Ministry of Food decided that people could do with less fruit from abroad, so fruit imports were cut back to almost nothing. Bananas disappeared from the shops.

By the end of the war, imported bananas could no longer be found in the markets and shops.

*I had never [seen] or eaten a banana. Where I lived there was a prisoner-of-war camp behind us. One day I was walking to the shops when a prisoner called us to the fence and offered us three bananas (for my sister and my brother). Not knowing how to eat it we peeled the banana, ate the skin and threw the inner away.*

Children of the Blitz
*by Robert Westall*

# Eating Out

The government set up restaurants to replace bombed-out factory canteens and provide eating places for those whose homes had been destroyed by bombs.

Restaurant meals were not rationed during the war. Instead, restaurants received supplies of food to match the number of meals they regularly served. Anyone could now enjoy an off-ration meal without parting with any coupons. As a result, people ate out much more often than they did before the war.

Those who could afford it were enjoying restaurant meals of five or six courses. There were such wide-spread complaints about these 'luxury feedings' that by 1942 the Ministry of Food limited restaurant meals to one basic dish, which could be meat, fish, poultry, cheese or eggs, with a maximum charge of 5 shillings (25p in today's money).

During the heavy bombing of 1940, the government set up 'British restaurants' for workers in cities where eating places had been bombed and for those who had been bombed out of their homes.

By 1943, there were over 2,000 British restaurants serving about 600,000 meals a day. The meals were not expensive – 10 pence or 1 shilling per person (4p or 5p in today's money). But despite the friendly atmosphere, some people had little good to say about the British restaurant and its self-serve system.

*Even wartime difficulties did not make me enjoy this method of serving oneself: pick up the tray, slide it along the bars, receive a slop of meat (not too bad, but a bit gristly), far too much potato and gravy and masses of cabbage . . . The coffee was vile, so I left it.*

Mrs Milburn's Diaries:
An Englishwoman's
Day to Day Reflections

When bombs destroyed factory canteens, mobile canteen services took their place. As you can see from the photograph above, meals were sometimes served in very difficult conditions.

## MINCED STEAK

1½ tablespoons (22 ml) dripping
2 small onions, finely chopped
1 lb (450 g) minced steak
1 cup stock or water
salt and pepper
1 dessertspoon (12 ml) oatmeal

Melt the dripping in a saucepan. When smoking hot, stir in the finely chopped onion. Cook for a few seconds, then add the minced steak and brown carefully, stirring with a wooden spoon to prevent burning. Add the stock or water and salt and pepper to taste. Cover and simmer gently for about 45 minutes. Add the oatmeal and continue cooking till the oatmeal is ready. Serve on a hot dish garnished with snippets of toast. Serve with mashed potatoes and any green vegetable. Serves 4.

Be sure to ask an adult to help you when chopping onions and using the cooker.

# Celebrations

Christmas or birthday celebration meals could be dreary affairs on wartime rations; therefore, people tended to store food and bring it out to liven up these special occasions.

*Most people had a store cupboard of hoarded tins for the very special occasion: someone's leave, the birth of a baby, or the moment when life seemed so desperate that 'Let's live today because tomorrow we might be dead' seemed the only sensible philosophy.*

Talking about the War *by Anne Valery*

These children are enjoying a street party to celebrate the end of the war in Europe. People would save their food rations for months to be able to have special celebration meals like this.

## EGGLESS CHRISTMAS CAKE

4 oz (100 g) carrot, finely grated
2 tablespoons (30 ml) golden syrup
3 oz (75 g) sugar
4 oz (100 g) margarine
1 teaspoon (5 ml) bicarbonate of soda
$\frac{1}{2}$ teaspoon (2.5 ml) almond essence
$\frac{1}{2}$ teaspoon (2.5 ml) vanilla essence
4–6 oz (100–150 g) dried fruit
12 oz (300 g) self-raising flour
1 teaspoon (5 ml) ground cinnamon
1 small teacup milk, slightly warmed

Cook the grated carrot and syrup over a low heat for a few minutes. Cream the sugar and margarine until light and fluffy. Stir the bicarbonate of soda into the carrot and syrup mixture, then beat it into the sugar and margarine, using it as if it were an egg. Stir in the flavourings and dried fruit. Fold in the flour and the cinnamon and add the warmed milk to make a moist dough. Put into a greased cake tin. Smooth the top and make a deep hole in the centre with a spoon, to stop the cake from rising too much during cooking. Put it into a hot oven, (220°C, 425°F, gas mark 7) then turn down to a very low heat (150°C, 300°F, gas mark 2) and bake for 3 hours.

People would often do without during the week in order to have enough food for a traditional Sunday lunch.

In the summer of 1940, the Ministry of Food banned the use of icing on wedding cakes in an effort to reduce the demand for sugar. Shops began to hire out cardboard cakes decorated with chalk icing sugar. The real cake, which was much smaller, would be underneath the cardboard cover.

# The War ends, but Rationing goes on

On 8 May 1945, Britain was celebrating VE Day (Victory in Europe). The war had ended, but not the shortages. In the years immediately following the war, a general world food crisis and harsh weather conditions resulted in rationing that was even stricter than in the war years. In 1946, the weekly rations for margarine, butter and cooking fat were even below the wartime level, and in 1948 the bacon ration was cut by half. Bread rationing began in July 1946; potato rationing began in 1947. However, there was a happy day for British children in 1953 when sweets were at last declared off ration.

**Above** Victory celebrations in London on VE Day.

Although the war was over, the food queues were still part of everyday life in Britain.

*The scramble for food occupies the foremost place in our lives today . . . prices of vegetables are soaring.*

Newspaper report, 1947

Rationing continued until 1954, nine years after the war was over. But the need to skimp and save had become so much a part of everyone's life that the effects lasted long after rationing had ended.

*The habit of hoarding every stringy runner bean and giant marrow persists in many of today's 70 year olds; nor can they restrain a look of horror if they should chance to see whole cartons of fried chicken thrown away in the gutter.*

Ration Book Recipes
*by Gill Corbishley*

These woman are putting their names on a petition in protest against further ration cuts. The petition was handed in to the Minister of Food in 1946.

## VICTORY SPONGE

1 large raw potato, grated
2 medium raw carrots, grated
1 cup breadcrumbs
1 tablespoon (15 ml) self-raising flour
2 tablespoons (30 ml) sugar
½ teaspoon (2.5 ml) vanilla or lemon essence
1 teaspoon (5 ml) baking powder
3 tablespoons (45 ml) jam

Mix together the grated potato and carrots, breadcrumbs, flour, sugar and flavouring. Thoroughly stir in the baking powder. Put the jam in a heated basin and spread it around to cover the inside of the basin. Cool. Put in the pudding mixture, tie on a cover of margarine paper, and steam for 2 hours.

Ask an adult to help you steam the sponge.

# Glossary

**Allotments** Areas of land, usually in a town, that people can rent for growing vegetables.

**Anderson shelter** A bomb shelter made from sheets of corrugated steel that were bolted together, dug into the ground and covered with earth. Many people had Anderson shelters in their back gardens during the war.

**Black market** A place or a system of illegal buying and selling of goods, such as food, that are under government control or in short supply.

**Blackout** A period when no light was allowed to escape from windows, doors, street lighting or car headlights so that towns could not be seen at night by enemy aircraft.

**Calorie** A unit of energy value in food.

**Campaign** A series of organized, planned activities that are designed to achieve a specific purpose.

**Diet** The food a person usually eats.

**Dripping** The fat that runs out of meat during roasting and is used for cooking or as food.

**Evacuate** To move from an area considered to be dangerous to a safe place. During the Second World War, children were evacuated from towns and cities that were likely to be bombed to the safety of the countryside.

**Evacuees** People who have been evacuated.

**Gunnybag** A sack made of coarse, heavy material.

**Import** To bring goods into a country from another country.

**Kilner jars** Large glass jars with tight lids.

**Lend-Lease Agreement** An agreement whereby the USA supplied food and equipment to Britain as a loan, which did not have to be paid back until after the war.

**Malnutrition** A condition in which the diet is lacking the kinds of food that are needed to maintain health.

**Moat** A deep, wide ditch surrounding a castle or house.

**Nutrients** Substances in food that help provide nourishment and keep you healthy.

**Petition** A document that outlines a specific request or complaint that is signed by many people and presented to a person in a position to do something about it.

**Prisoner of war** A member of the armed forces who is captured in war and held prisoner.

**Purée** Food that has been blended or mashed to a thick liquid.

**Rationing** Sharing out food or other goods in fixed amounts.

**Rissoles** Small fried cakes or balls of cooked minced food, especially meat.

**Slum** An area of a city that is overcrowded and where the houses are in such poor condition they are unfit to be lived in.

**Smithfield** The main London meat market.

**Surreptitiously** Trying not to be seen or heard.

**Torpedo** A cigar-shaped missile that is fired underwater from ships and explodes when it hits its target.

**U-boats** German naval submarines.

# Books to Read

*Children of the Blitz: Memories of Wartime Childhood* compiled by Robert Westall (Penguin Books, 1987)
*Growing up at War* by Maureen Hill (Armada/Collins, 1989)
*The Home Front* by Stewart Ross (Wayland, 1990)
*How We Used to Live* by Freda Kelsall (Macdonald/Yorkshire TV, 1987)
*The Home Front series: The Home Front 1939–1945; The Blitz; Evacuation; Prisoners of War; Rationing; Propaganda; Women's War* by Fiona Reynoldson (Wayland, 1991)

# Acknowledgements

Grateful acknowledgement is given for permission to reprint copyright material:

**Pages 8, 24, 33, 39** *Children of the Blitz* by Robert Westall (Penguin, 1987)

**Page 11** *We Were There in the 1940s* by Rosemary Rees (Heinemann)

**Page 15** *The Sheltered Days* by Derek Lambert (André Deutsch, 1965)

**Pages 25, 36** *The Wartime Kitchen and Garden* by Jennifer Davies (BBC, 1993)

**Pages 28, 42** *Talking about the War* by Anne Valery (Michael Joseph, 1991)

**Page 29** *Kitchen Front Recipes and Hints* by Ambrose Heath (1941)

**Page 31** *The World Is a Wedding* by Bernard Kops (Valentine, Mitchell and Co, 1973)

**Page 37** *A People's War* by Peter Lewis (Thames Methuen, 1986))

**Page 38** *When I Was Young* by Neil Thomson (Watts)

**Page 41** *Mrs Milburn's Diaries: An Englishwoman's Day to Day Reflections* (Harrap, 1979)

**Page 43** *Ration Book Recipes: Some Food Facts 1939–45* by Gill Corbishley (English Heritage, 1990)

**The Recipes**
Apply jelly, macaroni and bacon dish, quick vegetable soup, carrot cookies, cheese pudding, eggless sponge, uncooked chocolate cake, victory sponge, corned beef from *We'll Eat Again – A Collection of Recipes from the War Years* by Marguerite Patten (Hamlyn, 1985)
Potato piglests, eggless Christmas cake from *The Wartime Kitchen and Garden* by Jennifer Davies (BBC, 1993)
Skirly-mirly, minced steak from *Cooking in Wartime* by Elizabeth Craig (The Literary Press)
Crunchies from *Ration Book Recipes: Some Food Facts 1939–45* by Gill Corbishley (English Heritage, 1990)
Liver savoury from *The Daily Mirror,* 16 August 1940
Marrow pudding, parsnip pudding from the Guernsey Occupation Museum
Welsh Rarebit from Ministry of Food leaflet 'How to Use Stale Crusts'

While every effort has been made to trace copyright holders, the Publishers apologize for any inadvertent omissions.

# Index

Entries in **bold** refer to the pictures.